M000284535

DARING TO TAKE UP SPACE

DANIELL KOEPKE

THOUGHT CATALOG Books

THOUGHTCATALOG.COM
NEW YORK · LOS ANGELES

THOUGHT
CATALOG
Books

Copyright © 2019 Daniell Koepke. All rights reserved.

Published by Thought Catalog Books, an imprint of the digital magazine Thought Catalog, which is owned and operated by The Thought & Expression Company LLC, an independent media organization based in Brooklyn, New York and Los Angeles, California.

This book was produced by Chris Lavergne and Noelle Beams. Art direction, layout and design by KJ Parish with illustrations by Meni Chatzipanagiotou. Special thanks to Bianca Sparacino for creative editorial direction and Isidoros Karamitopoulos for circulation management.

Visit us on the web at thoughtcatalog.com and shopcatalog.com.

Made in the USA, printed in Saline, Michigan.

ISBN 978-1-949759-06-8

This is for the 17-year-old Daniell who was convinced she was worthless; who was convinced she would never survive or amount to anything. This is for the friends and family who never stopped believing in and supporting her. This is for all the people who feel that they have to shrink and hide who they are in order to be loved and accepted and worth something. This is for anyone who needs a reminder that you deserve to take up space in the world and that you are enough.

COMBATTING SHAME

The fact that you're struggling
doesn't make you a burden.
It doesn't make you unlovable or
undesirable or undeserving of care.
It doesn't make you too much
or too sensitive or too needy.
It makes you human.

Everyone struggles. Everyone has a difficult
time coping, and there are
days when we all fall apart.
During those times, we aren't always easy
to be around, and that's okay.
No one is easy to be around one hundred
percent of the time. Yes, you may
sometimes be unpleasant or difficult.

And yes, you may sometimes do or
say things that make the people
around you feel helpless or sad.
But those things aren't all of who
you are, and they don't discount
your worth as a human being.

The truth is that you can be struggling
and still be loved. You can be difficult
and still be cared for. You can be less
than perfect and still be deserving of
compassion and kindness.

Forgive yourself.
Forgive yourself for what happened.
For the mistakes you made. For your poor choices.
For not showing up the way
you needed to. For not being the person
you wanted to be. You're human.
You did the best you could in the moment
given what you knew and what you had,
and that's all you can ask of yourself.
You're still learning. You're still finding
your way. That takes time.
And you're allowed to give yourself that time.
You're allowed to show up in the world imperfectly.
You're allowed to fail at
things you tried hard for. You're allowed
to realize you made the wrong decision.
You're allowed to be someone who's still
figuring out their path and their purpose.
You're allowed to forgive yourself.

You can't go back and change the decisions you've made, but
you can choose
what you do today. You can keep choosing,
again and again. You can start over.
And that's where your power is—in today.

So no more beating yourself up. No more
going over and over it again in your head
and torturing yourself with the past.
What happened is over, and all the shame and
self-hatred in the world won't undo that.
Today, you're starting over.
Today, you're moving forward
with the new knowledge and experiences you have.

Today, you can be the person you want to be and live the life
you want to live.
You're not a bad person.
You're not a disappointment or a failure.
You're just human.
And it's okay. You'll be okay.

No one has a perfect track record.
Every person on this planet has done things
they regret, said things they wish they could take back,
and failed at things they cared about.
You deserve the same compassion and kindness
you'd extend to anyone else.
Even if you "should have known better."
Even if there were lots of warnings.
Even if other people in your position made different choices.
Even if you made the same mistakes over and over again.
You're still capable and worth something.
You're still important and lovable and
deserving of your own forgiveness.

Even though things might seem irreparably broken and lost,
they aren't.
There's more than one way to live a life
that makes you happy.
What's happened in the past might dictate
some or a lot of where
your future goes, but it doesn't mean
you can't find a new way
or meet new people or build a life
that feels good in a different way
that's impossible to predict.
Life is resilient. You are, too.
Don't forget that.

———

There's no right or wrong way to feel, because feelings aren't good or bad—they're just information. That's it. Information to help you better navigate your world. They exist for you. Not as a barometer for self-worth. Not as a sign that you're weak or resilient. Not as evidence that you're succeeding or failing at life. They're just feedback designed to help you get what you need and survive.

They can be painful and devastating, and sometimes they can be illogical or based on distortions, but they're never wrong or shameful. Even if other people react differently. Even if you've been reacting this way for a long time. Even if there's no apparent reason for you to feel the way you do—your feelings are important and valid. There's no judgment attached. It's just information.

When you feel overwhelmed, it's a sign that you need to take a break, make more time for self-care, or change up the way you're tackling your responsibilities. When you feel depressed, it's a sign that you're in a situation that feels hopeless and you're lacking in the resources necessary to successfully navigate your struggle and feel in control of your environment.

When you're still having a reaction to something
upsetting that happened a long time ago, it means
that you need to do more work processing that trauma
and that you need more effective coping mechanisms.

When you feel anxious about something, it means you
haven't yet acquired the experience
and evidence necessary
to show you that you can do the scary thing and be okay.
It doesn't mean you'll never get that evidence or that
you'll struggle forever—just that this is
where you are right now.

You don't need to beat yourself up. And you don't have to
feel ashamed. You just have to listen.
Listen to what your body is telling you, and use that
information to help you grow and get
what you need and navigate the world in a way that feels best
for you. You aren't failing and you aren't inadequate—you're
just collecting information. Your information is allowed to
look different than other people's information.
And no matter what anyone else feels,
your emotions are important
and your experience is valid.

You don't have to be productive to be worth something.
Doing more doesn't make you better or smarter or more
valuable. And taking a break doesn't make you lazy.

It makes you human. No one can endlessly
work without needing time to decompress.
No one is always going and doing and creating.
Every person needs quiet moments and slow days.
Days when you don't have energy to do anything
more than just exist.
And you're allowed that. You're allowed to rest.
You're allowed to slow down and breathe.
To have days where you aren't working
toward some greater purpose or plan.

Resting is productive in its own right. You can't be successful
if you're running on empty.
And you can't give the best version
of yourself if you're constantly neglecting your self-care.
There's strength in being someone
who honors what they need to cope and survive.
Strength in honoring your seasons and giving yourself
permission to shed everything you're carrying
for a moment so that you can bloom at a later time.

You deserve to rest if you need it. You deserve to have days
reserved for doing nothing. Even if other people with your
same struggles did more. Even if you "could have" pushed
yourself a little harder. Even if you took a break yesterday.
Whatever you manage to do today is enough.
No matter what, you're enough.

There's nothing shameful about being sensitive.
It doesn't make you weak or inadequate or too much.
It just means you experience the world a little more intensely. And that doesn't have to be a bad thing.

There's strength in being soft.
Strength in being raw and open and affected.
It might translate into more hurt and heartbreak, but it also translates into deeper love and meaning and relationships. It gives you greater insight into who you are and what you need to feel whole.
It increases your capacity for kindness and compassion and empathy.
It makes you intimately connected to the things and people around you. It lets you notice things other people miss and love in ways other people often don't know how to share.
It's your light, and it's a gift. And you don't owe it to anyone to hide that part of who you are.

You aren't a burden. Your feelings aren't wrong and your reaction isn't too much.
You're exactly the way you're meant to be.
You're sensitive and still worthy.
You're emotional and still valid.
You hurt and you feel and you struggle, and you're still enough.

Everyone navigates the world differently.
Your way of feeling and experiencing is allowed to be different. It doesn't matter if another person wouldn't be upset over something that hurt you.
It doesn't matter if they can cope with a struggle that debilitates you or if they can move on from something that takes you a long time to process. Your sensitivity is valid.
It's human and normal. And giving yourself permission to honor your experience is never anything but brave.

The irritating thing about anxiety
is that you know it's irrational.
You know logically there's no reason to be afraid.
You know no one else reacts this way.
You know this "should" be easy.
But anxiety doesn't care about logic. It still feels debilitating
and terrifying, and all of the reason in the world isn't enough
to ease the feeling that you're going to die.

And that disconnect can be painful. It feels like shame and
humiliation and inadequacy. And it translates into the belief
that you're defective—but you're not.
You just have a brain that reacts more strongly to things.
And that isn't your fault. It doesn't
happen because you're broken or weak.
It happens because you have
a chemical imbalance
or because you have a history of experiences
that have literally reshaped and rewired your brain.

And that isn't dumb or shameful. It makes sense.
Your response is so valid
and understandable given that you have a brain
that can't accurately distinguish
between things that are harmless and
things that are threatening.

You're doing the best you can to navigate
having a highly sensitive
control system up there,
and that's all you can ask of yourself.
You don't need to beat yourself up for reacting differently
than other people. It's okay to struggle with these things.
It's okay to feel anxious
about situations that don't bother other people.
It's okay if it takes longer to adapt to situations outside
your comfort zone. It's okay if you aren't able to adapt at all.
You aren't pathetic or weak—your brain is just different.
And it's okay. Different is okay.

It's a lie to think that you don't deserve love if you
aren't able to love yourself. You deserve it.
You deserve companionship and care and relationships
that feel good and spaces where you're cherished and valued.
Even if you have days where you want to crawl out of your skin
and disappear. Even if there are moments when you feel
inadequate and unlovable. You don't have to be alone
just because you're battling your own darkness.

Carrying that weight doesn't make you defective or too much
or unworthy of love and belonging. It makes you human.
It makes you someone who's internalized
judgments that were never yours to carry.
It makes you someone who's survived a
lifetime of trauma and loss and pain.
Someone resilient and inconceivably brave.
Someone courageous enough to connect,
despite the lies in your head. And there's no shame in that.

So please, don't withdraw or close yourself off.
Self-hatred doesn't get unlearned through isolation.
It's unlearned through love. Through connection and care.
Through having relationships and gathering evidence that
you can be imperfect and struggling and still be valued.
That you can hurt and be at war with your head and still
be wanted. I know it's hard to trust, but you belong.
And no matter how much darkness you're carrying,
you deserve to love and be loved.

You don't have to wait until you're in a crisis to deserve help.
It's something you're always allowed
to ask for if you're struggling.
Even if you know you'll be able to pick yourself back up
off the floor. Even if other people have it much worse.
Even if certain people don't understand or agree.
You don't have to be the sickest or the saddest to warrant
getting help. It's okay to be functional and still need support.
That isn't weakness or failure, and it isn't greedy.
It's human. And beyond that, it's smart.
It's proactive. It's self-advocacy and self-care,
and it's so incredibly valid.

Because you don't have to do everything on your own.
You're allowed to depend on other people.
You're allowed to be carried. You're allowed to have
limitations and needs. There's not a single person on this
planet who can navigate everything by themselves.
We're in this life together, tethered to each other, fumbling
and trying to find our way—and we all need help sometimes.
We aren't meant to go at it alone. And you aren't meant
to struggle in silence.

Your trauma is valid.
Even if other people have experienced “worse.”
Even if someone else who went through the same
experience doesn’t feel debilitated by it.
Even if it “could have been avoided.”
Even if it happened a long time ago.
Even if no one knows.
Your trauma is real and valid, and
you deserve a space to talk about it.
It isn’t desperate or pathetic or attention-seeking.
It’s self-care. It’s inconceivably brave. And
regardless of the magnitude of your struggle,
you’re allowed to take care of yourself
by processing and unloading some of
the pain you carry. Your pain matters.
Your experience matters. And your
healing matters. Nothing and no one
can take that away.

—

Having a mental illness doesn't make you weak or defective.
It just means that your brain functions differently.
It means that certain things are lacking or not working
the way they're supposed to. And that has nothing to do
with you or your worth. It's not your fault.
It's not something you chose. And it's not even entirely
within your control. It's an illness.
And in the same way that you wouldn't put down someone
with a broken leg for not being able to walk,
it doesn't make sense to put yourself down for not
being able to function the way other people can.

Your brain works a little differently, and so your ability
to navigate life and all the obstacles it presents
is going to look a little different, too. And it's okay.
It's okay that you experience the world differently.
It's okay that you have different needs and limitations.
It's okay that things that are easy for other people
feel unbearably difficult for you.
It makes sense, and it's valid.

You can't make comparisons,
because other people are not you.
You're doing the best you can to cope and survive,
and that's all you can ask of yourself.
It's enough. On your good days. On your bad days.
On the days you want to give up.
You're here, living and breathing and trying,
and you're enough.

Difficult is not synonymous with being a burden. Everyone has things about them that are hard for other people to navigate. Every person has quirks or personality traits or life challenges that take a toll on the people in their lives. And that isn't your fault. It isn't some moral failing or inadequacy. It's a normal, inevitable part of interpersonal relationships. It's part of what it means to be a human, and it's okay. There's not a single person on this planet who is easy and wonderful to be around one hundred percent of the time. So it's not fair to expect yourself to be some uncomplicated paragon of perfection every moment of every day, either.

You're human and you're imperfect and wired to be a pain sometimes, and it's okay. You are okay. And no matter what darkness you carry or how many difficult traits you might harbor, you're still deserving of kindness and human relationships. No matter what scars you wear or which hard truths you own, you're still deserving of love.

Babies are difficult, but parents still love them fiercely. Pets can misbehave and be hard to handle, but as owners, we still love and adore them. Partners and family can be frustrating and annoying, but that doesn't erase their good qualities or all the ways they make our hearts smile. It doesn't make us wish they weren't in our lives. And it doesn't diminish our worth.

You deserve the same level of compassion and kindness you'd extend to anyone else. You can be annoying and still be adored. You can be hard to handle on some days and still be loved. You can be struggling and less than perfect and still be wanted and cared for. The less pretty parts of who you are don't discount the ones that make you irreplaceable.

Stop minimizing and discounting your feelings.
You have every right to feel the way you do.
Your feelings may not always be logical, but
they're always valid. Because if you feel something,
then you feel it, and it's real and true for you.
It's not something you can ignore or wish away.
It's there, gnawing at you, tugging at your core,
and in order to find peace, you have to give yourself
permission to feel whatever you feel.
You have to let go of what you've been told you
"should" or "shouldn't" feel, because there is no
"should" when it comes to feelings.
You feel what you feel, and it's okay.
Your feelings can't be wrong because they're yours.
Not your partner's. Not your friends'.
Not your family's or your peers' or your coworkers'
or random strangers' you meet in passing.
They're yours. And you don't need anyone's
permission or approval to feel them.
Your feelings are important and they matter.
You matter—and it's more than okay to feel
what you feel. Don't let anyone, including yourself,
convince you otherwise.

The unfortunate, often painful, truth about life is that you can try your best at something and still not succeed. Even if you practice and put in hours of trial and effort and energy. Even if you receive support and guidance. Even if you retrace all the steps others have walked to reach their success—you can have all the heart and potential in the world and still lose. And that's okay. It's heavy and it's heartbreaking, and it's a memory that can ache for a lifetime, but it's okay. It doesn't mean you're incapable or a failure.
It means you're human.

It might mean that you were up against impossible odds or barriers that were deliberately put in place to keep people down and out, barriers that you have no control over, barriers that aren't your fault. But more often than not, it just means that you're destined or wired for something different.

Sitting with the truth that skill and effort do not guarantee success can be terrifying and demoralizing, but if there's one piece of comfort I can offer you, it's the reminder that all of the people before you who tried and failed—they survived and found their way. Maybe not immediately. Maybe it took months or years. Maybe it took trying and failing ten or twenty more times. Maybe they never found their way and are still wandering. But wherever they ended up, they're okay. The rejection that seemed like a death sentence in the moment didn't prevent them from finding a new path. The failure that seemed like a roadblock, that made them convinced they would be stuck forever, didn't stop them from being able to pursue the things closest to their heart. When you try your hardest and still lose, it won't stop you, either. It won't be the end of you. Life is unpredictable and resilient. You are resilient. And when doors close and people leave, it means you can open new doors. It means you have room for new people and new ways of being. No misstep or loss is strong enough to break your life.

You may feel like you're failing at recovery because you've been struggling for so long—but you're not. Recovery isn't a straight road. It isn't something that happens over the course of a few days or months, or even a few years. It's a path lined with ups and downs and roadblocks and dead ends. It's difficult and painful and exhausting. And it takes time. It takes time to unlearn the negative beliefs you've internalized. And it takes time to learn how to exist without using the behaviors you've depended on your whole life to survive.

So if you're feeling stuck right now, know that this is a part of your process. Know that it's normal and not anything you need to be ashamed of. The fact that you're still struggling doesn't mean you're going to be battling this forever. It just means that you have some more work to do. And that's okay.
You aren't broken or hopeless. You're wounded, but you can heal. You're healing right now.
So trust that you will get where you need to be when it's time. You're doing the best you can to cope and make it through each day, and it's enough.
No matter where you are in your recovery, you are enough.

Stop comparing where you are
with where everyone else is.
Everyone has their own unique journey.
A path that's right for someone else
won't necessarily be a path that's right for you.
And that's okay.
Your journey isn't right or wrong,
or good or bad.
It's just different.
Your life isn't meant to look like anyone else's
because you aren't like anyone else.
You're a person all your own
with a unique set of goals, obstacles, dreams, and needs.
So stop comparing and start living.
You may not have ended up where you intended to go.
But trust, for once, that you have ended up where
you needed to be. Trust that you are in the right place at
the right time. Trust that your life is enough.
Trust that you are enough.
Their path is theirs and yours is yours.
You're doing the best you can to navigate the unique
obstacles life has thrown at you
and to find your way despite them.
And that's all you can
ask of yourself.

Give yourself permission to be a beginner.
Everyone starts somewhere, and every person who is really
great at what they do was once someone
who didn't know much and struggled.
And you're allowed that.
You're allowed to be a person who
doesn't have all the answers yet.
You're allowed to be imperfect
and make mistakes and not have all the tools.
It takes time to build skills. It takes time to learn
how to navigate new things and develop your strengths.
Struggling at something you've never done before
is human and normal—and it's okay.
You aren't a failure if it's overly difficult.
You aren't pathetic or incompetent or shameful.
You're a beginner. You're still learning.
And there's honor in that.
Honor in opening yourself up to new
experiences and knowledge.
Honor in putting yourself outside your
comfort zone so that you can grow into a new,
more full version of yourself.
So if you're feeling lost and unprepared, know that it's okay.
Everyone else has been here before,
and they all made it through.
You'll figure everything out along the way. It takes time.
And you're allowed to give yourself that time.
It won't be this overwhelming and difficult forever.

There are no "shoulds" when it comes to
your ability to navigate the world.
You are where you are, and the things
that are hard for you are the things
that are hard for you. And it's okay.
It's okay that you're struggling.
It isn't evidence that you're weak or a failure.
It's human and it's normal
and it makes so much sense
given everything you have going on.
You're allowed to be vocal about what you're going through.
You're allowed to process your pain
in places other than your head.
You're allowed to be someone who
doesn't have it together every day.

I know that you're carrying so much shame.
I know that you feel alone and invisible.
That you're starving for connection and also terrified that
you'll be rejected or abandoned
if you let people see all of who you are
and where you are at.
But I hope you can trust that the right people
see you as more than the pain you hold.
That they don't expect you to
entertain or inspire them, or to be happy all the time.
That they've chosen you for you
and all that comes with you.

You can have dark days and still be wanted.
You can carry around a lot of pain and darkness
and still be enough. Those things are only
one part of you—they don't erase your light.

—

You don't have to be carrying the heaviest burden
for your struggle to matter.
It doesn't matter if other people have it "worse."
It doesn't matter if they've lost more or hurt for longer.
It doesn't matter if someone with your same struggle
is more debilitated or has less resources.
If something is painful for you, then it's painful for you.
And if it affects you, it's important and it matters.

There's no rule that only the person with the worst possible circumstances gets to vocalize their pain. Your struggle isn't "easier" or "more difficult." It's just different because people are different. You have different strengths and limitations and access to resources. You have a different history and lived experience. Your tolerance for hardship is allowed to look different. Pain is pain. No matter what it looks like. And no matter how your experience compares to anyone else's your feelings are valid and your struggle is still real.
Even if your life holds a lot of beauty.
Even if your cup is full and your days are blessed.
You're allowed to be affected.
You're allowed to hurt.
You're allowed to feel broken and sad.
And you deserve a space to talk about it.
Always.

I know that it feels like your entire life
is hanging on certain decisions.
That moving forward feels terrifying
because you don't want to
make the wrong choice.
That you can't make the wrong choice.
Because if you do—if you walk down
this path and things don't
work out—your entire life
will fall apart and you'll never be able
to go back and undo the damage.

But the truth is that the decisions in your life
don't have to be all or nothing.
There aren't only two options, and the options
don't have to be limited to
"you succeed and experience joy"
or "you fail and experience pain."

Life is fluid. It's unpredictable and always changing.
And it's resilient. No single choice is strong enough
to make or break your life.
Nothing you choose has to be the end of you.
You can always walk down a different path.
You can always close doors that don't serve
you and open new ones that do.
You never have to stay stuck.
There are always options.

Your life doesn't have to be an adventure full of excitement
and new experiences and beauty to be meaningful
and worthwhile. It can be quiet
and mundane and unremarkable
and still be valuable and deserving of pride.
Even if you're home most of the time.
Even if you're sick or struggling and stay in bed.
Even if you go through the motions every day.
Even if you don't go new places or experience new things.
Your life is still important and worth living.
It's okay to just "be." It's okay for things to be
unexciting and routine. To have smaller, quieter,
less sharable moments of happiness. It's okay
and it's normal and it's what everyone else's life
looks like most of the time.

So whatever you did today, please trust that it was enough.
Whatever you're able to do tomorrow, it will be enough.
However you navigate the world over the course of your life,
and whatever part you play in it, you are enough.

—

Whatever journey you're on or struggle you're working through, you'll get to where you want to be. It doesn't matter if you go more slowly than other people. It doesn't matter if you slip and fall and make mistakes that take you backwards. What matters is that you're here and trying. And that's all you can ask of yourself.

There's nothing written in stone that says certain accomplishments have to be achieved by a specific age or time frame. You're allowed to go at your own pace. You're allowed to have a journey that looks different than other people's. You're allowed to go more slowly or faster or take a completely different path altogether. That isn't weakness. It's you honoring your unique needs, and it's so okay and valid.

Forward is forward. You're taking steps every day to get to where you want to be, and it's enough.
No matter how fast or slow you go,
you're enough.

You are more than whatever burden you carry.
That pain might be a part of you,
but it isn't the only part, and it's definitely not
the part that matters most.
You're not your depression or your
anxiety. You're not your addictions or your illness.
You're not the person who's reluctantly single
or sad or can't seem to get it together.
You're not your body or whatever
baggage you carry.

You are your strengths and the things
you feel passionate about and the people
you would sacrifice everything for.
You are your smile and the way you laugh
and how you make other people feel.
You are your favorite books and films and the
songs that soothe your soul and bring you to tears.
You are the things you dream about and hope for and
all the steps you take every day to try to get there.

You're imperfect and you struggle and you can be difficult
for the people in your life, but you're still worthy of love
and kindness and belonging. The hard parts of who you are
and what you struggle with don't discount all the other parts.
And the right people know this. You aren't defective or
too much. You're human, and there is so much more
to you than the darkness you feel.

Your needs don't make you too much.
They don't make you selfish or weak or inadequate.
They make you human. We all have needs.
And they all look different because people are different.
We all have unique temperaments and traumas;
unique strengths and struggles and stories;
nuances that inform who we are and what we need
to survive and feel seen and heard—and they're allowed
to be different. Your needs are your needs, and no matter
what anyone says, they're valid.

So if you start to get caught up in comparisons, know that
it's okay if your needs don't look the same as someone else's.
And know that it's okay to ask for what you need.
Making your needs known isn't demanding or selfish.
It's self-care. It's about creating a space that's conducive
to your growth and well-being. It's about giving yourself
permission to exist in a way that honors your feelings and
your history. And more than anything, it's about
honoring yourself.

There's a lot of talk about just showing up
and trying your best. But it's important to recognize that
your "best" doesn't mean delivering your top performance.
It means giving all you can give without compromising
your health or hurting yourself. It means pushing yourself
while still knowing your limits and honoring where you are.
And that isn't weakness or failure. It's smart and it's self-care
and it's human—and that's okay. It's okay if the best you can
offer in any given moment isn't the same
as someone else's best.
We're all in different places and we all grapple
with a unique set of struggles and limitations.
Your best is allowed to look different.
It often will. And no matter how much it deviates from people
around you, what you're able to give is still valid and valuable.

There's quiet strength in being gentle with yourself.
Strength in withholding some of your effort and energy
if it means knowing that you're choosing self-care
and survival over self-sabotage and a mental breakdown.
Life is hard and you're allowed to show up imperfectly.
You're going to do the best you can in each moment
with where you are and what you have, and it's enough.
You are enough.

You can choose the wrong job or partner
or career and still find your way back
to a path or person that
makes your heart full.
You can make a decision that
takes you off-course and results in
missed connections and opportunities
and still create a life that
honors your hopes and dreams.
Maybe it honors them differently.
Maybe it doesn't happen the way you originally wanted.
Maybe it takes longer or you have to struggle a little more to get there. But that doesn't mean everything will be ruined. No matter what you choose or where you go, you can find your way. You will find your way. There are endless paths and possibilities. There is more than one way for you to be happy and live a good life.

Anxiety is a mental illness.
It's not something you chose,
and it's not entirely within your control.
It takes years of work and practice
and exposure to learn how to
challenge your anxious thoughts,
face your fears, and sit with the
discomfort they bring up.
And if you haven't gotten there yet, it's okay.
It takes time, and you're allowed to give yourself that time.
But more than that, you're allowed
to treat yourself with compassion.
You're allowed to give yourself a little more time
and go a little more slowly.
You're allowed to feel and react differently.
You're allowed to have different needs.
That doesn't mean giving up
or resigning to living your life in fear.
It means confronting your fears
at your own pace and in a way that
honors your needs and well-being.

486 | 9781949759068 | 486

Location: CB-3

ZBM I5VDH

Title	[illegible]
Cond	[illegible]
Date	[illegible]
mSKU	[illegible]
vSKU	[illegible]
unit_id	[illegible]
Source	[illegible]

[illegible]

[illegible]

XXXXX

You're doing what you can and showing up
in the ways you know how, and if that's the best
you can do in the moment, it's valid and enough.
Even if you submit to your anxiety.
Even if you struggle more than you succeed.

CONNECTION

It's easy to feel uncared for when people
aren't able to communicate
and connect with you in the way you need.
And it's so hard not to
internalize that silence as a reflection on your worth.
But the truth is that the way other people operate is not
about you. Most people are so caught up in their own
responsibilities, struggles, and anxiety
that the thought of asking someone else
how they're doing doesn't even cross their mind.
They aren't inherently bad or uncaring—
they're just busy and self-focused. And that's okay.

It's not evidence of some fundamental failing on your part.
It doesn't make you unlovable or invisible. It just means that
those people aren't very good at looking beyond their own
world. But the fact that you are—that despite the darkness
you feel, you have the ability to share your love and light
with others—is a strength.
Your work isn't to change who you are; it's to find people
who are able to give you the connection you need.
Because despite what you feel, you are not too much.
You are not too sensitive or too needy. You are thoughtful
and empathetic. You are compassionate and kind.
And with or without anyone's acknowledgment or affection,
you are enough.

Not everyone is going to feel a connection to you. And that's okay. It's not some personal failure or character flaw on your part. It doesn't make you worthless or unwanted. It just means that they're looking for something different. But different doesn't mean defective and it isn't a reason to hate yourself. It's the opinion of one person, or a few people, and it doesn't discount all of the people who do feel a connection to you. The people who adore the core parts of who you are. The people who aren't bored or apathetic. Who see all of you and don't want to turn away. And that's what you have to hold onto you.

I know that it's so hard to trust, but I promise
that there's nothing wrong with you.
You don't have to change who you are.
You don't have to shrink or disappear.
You just have to find your people.

And you have to accept that if the person
or group you want to connect with
consistently makes you feel invisible or
unwanted, it's probably a sign that they
aren't meant to be one of yours.
And that's okay. You will be okay.
There are people you haven't met yet
who will love you and fight for you.
Don't settle for anything less.

It's okay to say no. It's okay to say no to someone you love. It's okay to say no to someone who is angry or sad. To a friend. To a parent or child.
To relationships and sexual advances. To once-in-a-lifetime opportunities and people who are romantically interested in you.

Even if it hurts someone's feelings.
Even if you disappoint people. Even if you're judged or ostracized—it's okay to say no to anything and anyone that causes you pain or makes you uncomfortable.
You're allowed to put yourself first. You're allowed to set limits and boundaries. And you deserve to make your happiness and well-being a priority. You don't ever have to settle for something or someone that doesn't feel right.
And you definitely don't have to compromise yourself for the sake of making other people happy.
You have to take care of yourself, and if that means saying no, it's more than okay.

You don't need a reason for leaving a relationship.
You don't have to wait until things get bad or your partner does something awful to warrant ending it.
Wanting to leave is reason enough.
Being unhappy or unfulfilled and
disconnected is reason enough.
Even if they're smart and kind and successful.
Even if they're supportive and caring and have a huge heart.
Even if you have a long history
or they haven't done anything wrong.
You're not obligated to stay in any relationship that you don't want to be in. You don't owe it to anyone to maintain something that doesn't feel right.

Wanting to leave doesn't make you a bad person,
and breaking someone's heart doesn't make you terrible.
It makes you brave.
It's brave to honor your needs,
and it's even braver to give your partner
the chance to be with someone who can love them
in all the ways they deserve.

Trust your gut. Trust that if something feels off or empty or unfulfilling that you deserve to make a shift and let go. You aren't defective or incapable of love, and you aren't destined to be alone. You're human. You tried your best, and it didn't work out—and it's okay. Your partner will be okay. Maybe not today or tomorrow or six months from now, but they'll survive the storm. And you will, too. You're allowed to put yourself first. There are a lot of things in life we have to settle on, but your heart and happiness don't have to be among them. You get to choose. You get to leave if it doesn't feel right.

You're allowed to need more space
and alone time than other people.
You're allowed to take things more slowly.
You're allowed to set limits
on when and how often you communicate with people.
You're allowed
to turn down plans in order to focus on other responsibilities
or self-care.
You're allowed to say,
"I'm not going to engage with you if you say those things."
You're allowed to say, "These things don't feel good and
I'm not going to tolerate them."
Even if people get angry. Even if they
get disappointed or hurt or sad.
You deserve to set boundaries
and take care of yourself.

It doesn't matter if other people
don't need those things to feel okay.
You aren't other people.
You need what you need, and your needs
are important and valid.
And you shouldn't have to compromise
your self-care or safety or sanity
to make other people happy.
You are deserving of your own protection and care.
You deserve to exist under terms that feel good and
honor who you are and where you're at.
Don't shrink for anyone else's sake.
You're allowed to take care of yourself.

Not all toxic people are cruel and uncaring. Some of them love us dearly. Many of them have good intentions. Most are toxic simply because their needs and way of existing in the world force us to compromise ourselves and our happiness. They aren't inherently bad people, but they aren't the right people for us. And as hard as it is, we have to let them go. Life is difficult enough without being around people who bring you down, and as much as you care, you can't destroy yourself for the sake of someone else. You have to make your well-being a priority. Whether that means breaking up with someone you care about, loving a family member from a distance, letting go of a friend, or removing yourself from a situation that feels painful—you have every right to leave and create a safer space for yourself.

Not everyone has a heart like yours.
Most people will not give and give.
Most don't know how. All they know how to do is take.
Not because they mean to,
but because they never learned otherwise.
And so, carrying a heart this big can hurt.
It can leave you hollow
and hungry and exhausted.
And even though sharing so much of
your light is a gift, it can also start to feel like a curse.
But it doesn't have to be.
It's okay to be selective about who gets
your heart and time and energy.
It's okay to step back from people
who take more than they give.
Even if they have good intentions.
Even if there are some days when the effort is there.
Even if they love you and care.
It's okay to be particular about
the people you let into your life.
That isn't selfish or unkind.
It's self-care.
You can't share your time and energy with everyone.
You can't meet everyone's needs.
And you can't take care of people
every minute of every day. No one can. You're allowed to
turn people down and take time for yourself.
And you're allowed to prioritize your self-care.
You can't be there for the people you love
if your tank is empty. And you can't be there for yourself
if you've given all you have to give.

Forgiveness is not necessary for healing.
You don't owe it to anyone.
You don't have to make amends
with people who have made you
feel broken or abused or betrayed.
With people who have not just
once, but repeatedly, tried to tear you down
and make you feel small.
Even if they had good intentions.
Even if they're family.
You don't ever have to sacrifice yourself
for the sake of "being the better person."

Withholding your heart
doesn't make you selfish
or bad or unkind.
It makes you smart.
It makes you someone who values themselves.
It makes you someone brave enough
to stand by their boundaries.
Someone who honors their feelings.
Someone fiercely protective
of their self-care.

Because the truth is that
your healing should never be dependent
on bringing people who hurt you back into your space.
And more often than not, you can't heal by going back to
the relationships and dynamics that broke you.
So if forgiving someone feels too painful and invalidating,
know that you don't have to choose that path.
You're allowed to be selective.
You're allowed to put yourself and your healing first.

—

Your value isn't measured by your relationship to others.
Even if your circle is small or empty.
Even if you feel invisible to people.
Even if people have left.
Even if you're responsible for their leaving.
You're still worth something whether or not people
see and care for you.

You're a person.
You have feelings and hopes and dreams.
You have gifts that no one else can give
and insight that no one else can share.
You're here, living and trying despite it all;
showing up every single day, even when it's hard.
And that counts for something.
You don't have to be in a relationship or
romantically involved or surrounded by friends
to be someone who matters.
It's okay to be alone.
It's okay to have a smaller circle.
And it's okay to have a life that's a little quieter.
You're enough. Today and tomorrow and the day after that.
With or without anyone else, you're so incredibly enough,
and you matter.

It's okay to change your yes to a no.
Yeses aren't permanent. They're something
we choose again and again every day.
Something we have the right to recall and
reconsider as soon as saying yes no longer feels
conducive to our well-being and happiness.
Changing your yes to a no might make people
angry. It might hurt their feelings or cause them
to see you as a flake and result in lost connections.
But if saying no means staying true to yourself,
honoring your feelings, and making self-care
a priority, it's worth it. Don't let anyone
convince you otherwise.

You aren't difficult to love. You aren't too needy or too much.
You're just not for everyone. And that's okay.
It's human and it's normal.
Every person on the planet has parts of who they are that
are unattractive and unacceptable to certain people.
Every person is someone's idea of "hard to love."
But each of us also embodies traits and qualities that make
us perfect for someone else.
Each of us has struggles and pieces of our story that don't
frighten certain people and wouldn't push them away.
Pieces that make us exactly what they're looking for and
histories that never make them question our lovability
or worth. And that counts for something.

No matter how many people find you difficult to love, there
will always be others who feel like they've struck gold.
And no matter how many turn away, I hope you can trust
that there's nothing wrong with who you are.
That your needs are valid.
That you're inherently lovable and worthy of
relationships that don't hurt.

You're not for everyone,
and this doesn't have to be a bad thing.
You're rare and resilient and have
gifts to offer that can't be replicated.
You know who you are and what you need,
and you shouldn't ever have to settle for people
who love you poorly. There is better love out there waiting.
There are people better suited to hold your heart.
People you haven't met yet who will make you forget that
you ever doubted your value.
People who will laugh when they hear you say
you're difficult to love.
And if you haven't found them yet, you will.
Keep holding out. The love you're waiting for is coming.

It's not just okay to make self-care a priority—it's imperative.
You're allowed to put your needs first.
You're allowed to say no to people.
You're allowed to turn down plans and take longer
and go more slowly.
You're allowed to give yourself the majority
of your time and energy.
That isn't selfish and it doesn't make you a bad person.
It's self-care, and it's survival.
You don't owe it to anyone to sacrifice
what you need to cope and survive.
You can't pour from an empty cup.
You can't effectively take care of other people
if you aren't first taking care of yourself
and your own needs.
Your self-care is fundamental to being a
source of care and support for others.
Shrinking and ignoring
your needs helps no one.

Trust that it's okay to put your needs first.
You deserve to take care of yourself.
You deserve to have the time and space
and energy to get your needs met.
You deserve to exist under conditions that
feel comfortable and allow your
best self to come through.

You don't owe your family affection if they're being abusive and treating you poorly. I know that it's so difficult not to feel guilty for holding back that love. I know that there are people who will tell you that you should just grin and bear it because they're family.

People who will shame you for the way you feel. People who will try to convince you that wanting to take care of yourself in this way is selfish and unjustified. But the truth is that it's not your responsibility to be kind or loving to people who have consistently hurt and mistreated you—especially when these people continue to disregard your feelings, ignore your boundaries, and refuse to take responsibility for their behavior.

Just because the person hurting you is a family member doesn't make them an exception.

Choosing not to be affectionate with family who have abused or mistreated you doesn't make you a bad person. It isn't selfish or disrespectful—it's a form of self-care. It's about you honoring your feelings and holding people accountable for their abuse.

It's about you standing up for yourself and your needs. And it's about you making your mental health a priority. So if getting distance from certain family members is what you need right now or permanently, you have every right to withhold your love and leave. You don't have to sacrifice yourself for the sake of maintaining a relationship. And you don't ever have to apologize for creating a safer space for yourself.

It's important to be understanding and kind
with the people in our lives because no one is perfect,
and we all have days where we don't want to try;
days where we speak from our hurt or our ignorance
instead of our hearts. But relationships are a two-way
street, and you can't be the only one investing time
and energy into healing the hurt and restoring the connection;
you can't always be the one who gives and gives
but never gets back.

Apologies aren't enough. "I'm sorry" implies a
willingness to stop behaving in ways that hurt—but it
loses its value when a person reopens the same wounds
over and over again with no signs of change.

Know that you deserve reciprocity. You deserve
to have people in your life who are as thoughtful and
understanding with your heart as you are with theirs.
You deserve to say, "I care about you, but I can't accept
that anymore." Because if they don't care for your heart,
someone has to. And that someone has to be you.

Missing someone doesn't mean
you made the wrong decision in letting go.
It doesn't mean that deep down you're confused or unsure.
It doesn't mean you're destined to be together or that your
original feelings were misplaced.
It means that what you had was real.
That there there was love and genuine
connection and a bond that made an impact.
And that's okay.
It makes sense that you would miss them.
It makes sense that you would feel hurt and destroyed and sad.
Healing doesn't happen overnight.
It takes time to figure out how to navigate life without them.
Time to create a new routine
and find different people to fill your circle.
Don't run back just because you're feeling
the heaviness of that hole.
You let them go for a reason.
That reason hasn't changed just because
they're not in your life.
You can't go back to what broke you.
You can't sacrifice your sanity and self-care
for a momentary feeling of discomfort.
The sadness will pass. The hurt will fade.
New people will take their place and someday soon,
your heart will feel full again.
So when the longing gets heavy and you feel yourself
thinking about going back,
remember that it's okay to miss them.
It's okay to wish things could have worked.
And it's okay to keep walking.

—

Just because someone used to be an important part of your life doesn't mean you have to cling to the friendship when it begins to die. Your relationship was once something beautiful and fulfilling, and that's a wonderful thing. But at a certain point, no amount of watering and nurturing will bring it back to full bloom. The fact that it has deteriorated doesn't mean you're incapable of sustaining meaningful friendships. It doesn't mean you're not worth the time and effort it takes to maintain a connection. And it isn't any sort of evidence that you're a burden or a bad friend. It just means that the relationship has run its course. It means that you've evolved into different people or moved apart or just lost each other in the clutter and preoccupation of life's everyday demands. But it isn't a reflection on your value as a person and friend.

It's okay to mourn the loss of a relationship that used to have a special place in your heart. But if keeping yourself tethered to this person is causing more damage than healthy detachment and ongoing growth, it's also okay to stop watering the friendship and let it die out. You don't have to sacrifice your well-being for the sake of maintaining a relationship that doesn't serve you anymore. You're allowed to be picky when it comes to the people you let into your mental and physical space. You're allowed to conserve your time and energy only for people who reciprocate. Because you deserve to feel seen and heard and cared for. You deserve relationships that make you feel fulfilled and connected. And no matter how long of a history you have with a person, you deserve to let go of any friendship that hurts you and forces you to prove your worth.

You don't need anyone's affection or approval in order to be good enough. When someone rejects or abandons or judges you, it isn't actually about you. It's about them and their own insecurities or limitations or needs, and you don't have to internalize that. Your worth isn't contingent upon other people's acceptance of you.
It's something inherent.

You exist, and therefore you matter.
You're allowed to voice your thoughts and feelings.
You're allowed to assert your needs and take up space.
You're allowed to hold onto the truth that who you are is exactly enough. And you're allowed to remove anyone from your life who makes you feel otherwise.

Don't take on other people's baggage and pain.
Don't confuse the opinion of one person with the feelings of everyone. Don't let someone's limitations define the validity of your feelings and needs.
Don't put your self-worth in anyone's hands except your own.

—

Boundaries aren't selfish.
They aren't too much and they aren't weakness.
Boundaries are conditions that allow you to take care of yourself, conditions that give you the means to survive and keep from sinking.
They're circumstances that honor
your needs and respect your feelings.
Limits that you get to decide on;
limits that are inherently valid, no matter
how they compare to anyone else's.

You deserve to create a space for yourself
that feels safe and supportive.
You deserve to exist under terms
that don't harm you, terms that allow
your best self to come through.
Even if other people don't understand.
Even if it makes them feel angry or rejected or sad—
your boundaries are necessary and they matter.
Their needs matter, too, and it's not wrong
to want to make shifts to accommodate both.
But the truth is that you
can't take care of anyone else
if your own needs aren't being met.

You don't have to explain your boundaries.
You don't have to justify them,
and you don't need anyone's approval.
You need to believe that you're
someone worth taking care of,
and you need to trust that if anyone
is entitled to your protection and care, it's you.

—

Being single doesn't make you unlovable or unwanted.
You're allowed to be single.
You're allowed to be committed to yourself.
You're allowed to be alone.
Romantic love isn't the only love,
and it isn't the only love that matters.
There's beauty in investing time in yourself.
In learning who you are and what you need and filling your
tank with your own validation and reassurance.
There's beauty in friendships that have lasted a lifetime
and in connections that make you feel seen and heard
and understood.
Beauty in road trips with people you love and late night
talks where you share your whole heart.
Beauty in unbreakable sibling bonds and
unconditional love from family.
Beauty in sitting across from another human
and realizing how much you have in common.
In realizing that you aren't alone.
Just because you're single now
doesn't mean you'll be single forever.
But even if you are, there are other people outside of a
romantic relationship that you can share your life with.
There are other bonds that can make you feel fulfilled
and connected and loved.
You aren't one half of a whole.
You don't need someone to fix you or put you together.
And you don't have to wait for another person to live your
life. You're already complete.
Your life is already here, ready and waiting for you.
And with or without a partner, you're
already worthwhile and lovable and enough.

HOPE AND RESILIENCE

You have to let go of the life you could've had.
The life you would be living if you hadn't made
certain choices. If you hadn't let certain people
into your life or been in the wrong place at the wrong time.
Wishing for things to be different and beating yourself up for
the mistakes you've made won't change your circumstances.
It's happened, it's done, and this is where you are at.
And it's okay. You will be okay.

Your life isn't over—it's just going to be different.
And different doesn't have to mean bad. It just means you
have to become more creative with your self-care. It means
you have to find slightly different ways to navigate the world
and your relationships. And sometimes it means finding
new strengths—strengths that open new doors and doors that
lead to new passions and friendships and connections.
Doors that make you look back and smile for having doubted
the resiliency of life—for doubting your own resiliency.

You can't go back and change the past, but you can decide
how you live today. Your story isn't over yet.
There may be pain and struggle, but there are always ways
to make your time here meaningful and worthwhile.
It might take time, and it might challenge you,
but the light is there. There is always a way. I promise.

This work is not for nothing.
The nights you keep pushing forward,
even when you feel exhausted and overworked.
The days you continue to show up and try, even when it's uncomfortable and would be easy to quit.
All the opportunities you have to postpone and all things you have to sacrifice in order to move toward what's important to you.
It has a purpose. Some things take time to build.
And you're building.
You're building and planting the seeds, and you're growing.
Even when you feel stuck.
Even when the progression feels drawn out.
You're getting there, slowly, each and every day.
It's heavy, and the work is hard, but it's not for nothing.
You'll get to where you want to be and you'll become the person you want to become.
Or maybe, you'll blossom into a version of yourself you didn't even know you wanted or didn't know was possible.
You don't have to have all the answers.
You don't have to think about everything you need to do to get to the finish line.
You just have to focus on the most immediate thing
in front of you and do what you need to survive today.
This work will pay off.
And if it doesn't—if you end up somewhere else entirely-
know that the growth it took to get to wherever you landed is valuable in its own right.
So keep building. Keep taking it one day at a time.
Breathe. Things won't be this bard forever.
There's a point beyond this pain, and you'll get there.

Just because something is difficult
doesn't mean it's impossible.
Uncomfortable, yes.
Exhausting and overwhelming, yes.
But not impossible.
You've made it through similar struggles before.
You've survived every obstacle the universe has ever
thrown at you up until this point. So it's safe to say that
you can survive this, too.

You don't have to figure out everything today.
You don't have to solve your whole life tonight.
You just have to show up and try. Focus on
the most immediate thing in front of you.
You'll figure out the rest along the way.

It's okay to struggle. It's okay to feel overwhelmed.
And it's okay to make mistakes. You're still learning
how to navigate this new path. It's going to take time.
And you're allowed to give yourself that time.
All you have to do is show up and try.
It's always been enough before.
It will be enough this time, too.

—

Breathe. You're going to be okay.
Breathe and remember that you've
been in this place before.
You've been this uncomfortable and anxious
and scared—and you survived.
Breathe and know that you can survive
this too. These feelings can't break you.
They're uncomfortable and
debilitating and painful, but they won't last forever.
I know it hurts.
I know you feel like this is going to be the end of you,
but it will pass.
Maybe not immediately.
Maybe not today or tomorrow or a week from now.
But sometime soon, the feelings are going to fade,
and when they do, you' ll look back and laugh
for doubting your resilience.
For being so convinced that something so fleeting,
would last forever.
I know it feels unbearable, but you've been here before.
You survived it then, and you can survive it now.
Keep breathing, again and again.
This will pass. I promise it will pass.

Instead of focusing on how far you still have to go, take some time today to remind yourself of how far you've already come. Yes, you might still be struggling. And yes, you may still have some distance to cover, but those things don't discount the progress you've already made. Healing takes time. Life takes time. It's not a process that can be rushed. You'll get there when you get there. And you're allowed to give yourself that time.

Beating yourself up for not being further along does absolutely nothing to help get you closer to where you want to be. It makes you feel inadequate and ashamed, and it keeps you stuck. So stop fixating on how much farther you need to go and start acknowledging how incredible it is that you've gotten as far as you have. That despite how difficult this path has been, you haven't given up. That even though you've felt hopeless and defeated, you keep showing up every day and trying your best. Because that's what matters.

I know it can be so painful to feel stuck. I know you're tired. And I know that it's hard not to feel ashamed if it's taking you longer. But you have to let go of this idea that you should be further ahead. Trust that it's okay to be where you are. Trust that you won't be here forever. Trust that you will get to where you need to be in your own time. You're doing the best you can each day to fight the darkness you feel and take steps forward in your process, and that's all you can ask of yourself. It's enough. No matter where you are in your journey, you're enough.

When life gets hard, try to practice moving away from thoughts of "Why is this happening to me?" and "It's not fair" and "Everything is awful" to "How will this experience help me grow?" and "What does this struggle have to teach me?"

You can withdraw and wallow and feel sorry for yourself for having a hard life, or you can reframe the narrative. You can try to believe that your pain is teaching you how to survive and be resilient in the face of horrible discomfort. How to practice radical acceptance. How to hurt and be uncomfortable and live life anyway. How to become creative with your self-care and be a fierce advocate for yourself. How to relinquish the need for control and to trust the process.

Because perspective really is everything. There's so much we can't control in life when things go wrong, but we can control the stories we tell ourselves. We can choose which pieces of the puzzle to focus on and which ones to reframe. We can rewrite the narrative.
And there's so much power in that.

Not every struggle has, or should have, a lesson attached to it. And you shouldn't have to suffer in order to grow. It's also okay and valid to give yourself permission to grieve and feel angry and heartbroken about your circumstances, because that's part of healing.

But sometimes when you're feeling lost and helpless,
looking at your struggle as pain with a purpose
can help make it a little easier to bear.
So tell yourself a different story.
There are lessons you haven't yet learned and
benefits you haven't yet reaped.
This is not for nothing.

Life isn't always a pattern. Just because today is bad doesn't mean tomorrow will be. Just because you keep getting rejected doesn't mean you'll always be rejected. Just because things haven't worked out for a long time doesn't mean your life won't ever sort itself out or that you won't find that special person or get that job or reach that goal. Just because you've had a bad week or month or year doesn't mean you'll have a bad life.

Life is unpredictable. It takes time. Healing takes time. Overcoming obstacles takes time. It's not a process you can rush or control. And that can be terrifying because it means there might be bad things ahead that you can't prepare for. But it also means there might be some incredible things waiting for you that you would have never have imagined.

I know it's so hard to see it when you're stuck in a dark tunnel, but you have to trust that things won't be like this forever. What's happened so far doesn't have to dictate where you go. It's just one page or a few chapters in your book. It's not how the story ends.

And if you start to doubt that, think back to where you were a year ago, or two or five. What struggles were you facing that you felt convinced you could never overcome but did? Which goals did you feel certain you could never reach but were able to meet or succeed in your own time? So trust that something better is coming.
It has before, so many times.
It will this time, too.

Let whatever you do today be enough.
Let go of the judgment you have about what you
"should be" or "could be" doing and today,
allow yourself to just be.

Stop fixating on where everyone else is,
and try to give yourself permission
to be exactly where you are.
Quiet the voice telling you to do more and be more,
and trust that in this moment, who you are, where you're at,
and what you are doing is enough.

You'll get to where you need to be in your own time.
Until then, breathe. Breathe and be patient with yourself
and your process. You're doing the best you can to cope
and survive amid your struggles, and that's
all you can ask of yourself.
It's enough. You are enough.

—

When you find yourself drowning in self-hate, you have to
remind yourself that you weren't born feeling this way.
That at some point in your journey, some person or experience
sent you the message that there was something wrong with
who you are, and you internalized those messages and took
them on as your truth.
But that hate isn't yours to carry, and those
judgments aren't about you. And in the same way that you
learned to think badly of yourself, you can learn to think new,
self-loving, and accepting thoughts.
You can learn to challenge those beliefs, take away their
power, and reclaim your own.
It won't be easy, and it won't happen overnight.
But it is possible. And it starts when you decide that
there has to be more to life than this pain you feel.
It starts when you decide that you deserve to discover it.

You don't have to solve your whole life today.
You don't have to think about tomorrow or next week or three months from now. All you have to do is make it through today.

I know you feel helpless and hopeless and scared.
But I also know that if you look back at the past, there's so much evidence that you're more capable than you think. Evidence that you're impossibly resilient and brave and creative with your self-care.
Evidence that you always find a way.
That you always end up where you need to be.
That you've survived every hard moment and decision up until this point, and that you can survive this one, too.

Things might be painful and difficult for a long time, but your life doesn't have to be perfect for it to be meaningful and worthwhile.
You can feel uncomfortable and scared and overwhelmed and live life, anyway.

You can focus on what you can do instead of what you can't.
You can focus on the things you're doing well instead of the things you're doing poorly.
You can focus on the people who have stayed instead of wondering about the people who left.
You can focus on how far you've already come instead of beating yourself up for how far you still need to go.
You can give yourself permission to have an imperfect life marked by struggle instead of expecting it to be easy.

You aren't the things that haunt you.
You aren't the pain you feel.
You aren't defective or broken.
You're human; you're doing the best
you can, and you have so much more to offer the world than the demons you're fighting.
You'll find a way to keep going.
You'll find a way to make this life work.
And you don't have to do it alone.

GROWTH AND AFFIRMATION

Most of my life has been spent trying to shrink myself.
Trying to become smaller. Quieter. Less sensitive.
Less opinionated. Less needy. Less me.
Because I didn't want to be a burden. I didn't
want to be too much or push people away.
I wanted people to like me.
I wanted to be cared for and valued.
I wanted to be wanted.

So for years, I sacrificed myself for the sake of making
other people happy. And for years, I suffered.
But I'm tired of suffering, and I'm done shrinking.
It's not my job to change who I am in order to become
someone else's idea of a worthwhile human being.
I am worthwhile. Not because other people think I am,
but because I exist and therefore, I matter.
My thoughts matter. My feelings matter.
My voice matters. And with or without anyone's
permission or approval, I will continue to speak my truth.
Even if it makes people angry. Even if it makes them
uncomfortable. Even if they choose to leave.
I refuse to shrink.

I choose to take up space. I choose to honor my feelings.
I choose to give myself permission to get my needs met.
I choose to make self-care a priority.
I choose me.

—

You're not where you want to be. And it's okay. Everyone starts somewhere. This is where you are right now. It doesn't mean you'll be here forever. It doesn't mean you're stuck. It just means this is where you stand today. I know this journey feels so overwhelming. I know it feels impossibly long and difficult and painful. And I know there are days when it feels easier to give up. But the truth is that most things worth having don't come easy. Change takes time. Getting to a better place takes time. You aren't a failure because it's taking you so long or because you're struggling just to start. You aren't weak or incapable. You're human. This work is hard. It's uncomfortable and mentally and physically taxing and terrifying—and it makes sense that it would take you time. It makes sense that this is a struggle.

You don't have to solve your whole life overnight. And you don't have to feel ashamed for being where you are. All you have to focus on is one small thing you can do today to get closer to where you want to be. Slowly and lightly, one step at a time. You can get there. Every effort you make adds up over time. And you're capable of doing that work. So breathe and trust that it's okay to be here today. Trust that something better is coming. Trust that you have what it takes to get there.

Maybe we don't heal by convincing ourselves
that someday, the pain will fade;
that we'll return to our former selves
and reclaim the life we used to have.
Maybe we heal when we accept that
it's okay to never go back; when we stop trying
to use the broken pieces to rebuild the old picture
and instead create a new one.
Maybe we heal by affirming that even with this pain,
we can craft a life that gives us meaning;
that even when there are storms that floor our hearts,
we can learn how to swim; that when night falls,
we can learn to create our own light.
Maybe healing means trusting that no matter
how many times we have to recreate ourselves
and redirect our path, we will end up
where we are meant to be.

All transitions are scary and difficult in the beginning. And that's okay. It's human and it's normal. But the hard parts won't feel overwhelming forever.
Slowly, as time passes—as you get more practice and become more acclimated—the things that once felt unfamiliar and daunting will become your new routine, and they won't feel so scary anymore.

The discomfort will only be temporary. It will get easier with time. You will find a way to manage; you always have. And you don't have to manage on your own.
You're allowed to ask for help.
You're allowed to do things imperfectly.
You're allowed to give yourself time to adjust.

You've already survived and succeeded through so many transitions throughout your lifetime, so it's safe to say that you can survive and succeed this time, too.
You're so much more resilient and capable than you give yourself credit for. And even if things stay difficult, with time and practice you can become an expert at managing them. It will be okay. You will be okay.

There's no shame in taking longer.
You aren't behind, and your timing isn't wrong.
Your path is just different. And it's okay.
Life isn't a competition or a race.
You can't compare the journey you're on or the things you've achieved because everyone is going to different places.
We all have different goals and dreams and values.
Different strengths and struggles and traumas.
Different opportunities and access and resources.
And that means the places we get to and the ways in which we get there are going to be unique.

It's okay if your timeline looks different.
And it's okay to walk down a completely different path.
There's strength in honoring your needs.
Strength in giving yourself the best possible chance to succeed by going at your own pace and being mindful of what you're currently able to give.
You just have to be patient with yourself and your process.
You'll get to where you want to be.
You'll achieve your goals.
You'll make it to the end.
You have time.
There's nothing written in stone that says you have to reach certain milestones by a specific age.
There's no rule that your successes count less if you take longer to achieve them.
It takes however long it takes, and it's okay.
It's still real and worthwhile and valid.
You're allowed to take longer than other people.
You're allowed to take the time you need.

Something I often think about is how to cultivate happiness
and hope when your existence feels unbearably painful.
I'm learning that in the same way fixating on all the things
going wrong feeds depression and hopelessness,
noticing all the things that are still going right makes room
for hope and helps give you new strength.
And maybe that's all happiness
really is—just noticing the good things.
Noticing and collecting evidence that there are still people
who make your heart sing and places that call to you and
moments where you laugh or love so hard that for a few
moments, you forget about all the pain you carry.
So if things are hard today, just notice.
They don't have to be big things. Maybe the sun is shining
or a stranger smiled at you in passing. Maybe you heard
from an old friend or learned something new that changed
your perspective. Maybe someone checked in with you
when you felt invisible or they validated your feelings when
you felt alone. And if you can't think of anything,
create a moment for yourself. Reread your favorite quotes.
Look at an old photo that makes you smile. Listen to a song
that makes you feel alive. Do something that brings back
warm memories. Find a space that helps you feel grounded.
Watch the sunset. Call up a friend who makes you laugh.
And no matter how difficult things get, keep noticing.
Keep making lists and writing things down so that
you remember when there are hard days. Keep reminding
yourself that yes, there are painful moments, but there are
still good things and good people. There are still
opportunities for joy and love. There are still
reasons to keep trying.

What I've learned about shame is that it thrives in silence. That it lives and breathes and grows when the only person carrying its weight is you. But shame can't survive when it's out in the open. It can't survive when you speak it and own its presence. It loses its power when you realize that you can hold these hurts and traumas and still be enough. That you can struggle in ways that other people don't and feel broken in all the places you feel you should be whole, and still be loved and accepted and worthwhile.

Shame loses its power because it can be flipped on its head and challenged. Because you're given clear, irrefutable evidence that your fears about your worth are not truth. That your feelings are not fact.
That other people carry these weights, too, and that if you would extend your heart and kindness and compassion to someone else struggling in the same way, you deserve to bring that back home to yourself. You're not an exception.
You never have been. You never will be.

What do you want to be remembered for after you die? No one is going to sit at your funeral and recount how thin and beautiful you were. They're not going to tell stories about how big you got in the gym or what size you wore or how good you looked in pictures. At the end of your life, none of that will matter. What will matter is what you did and how you made people feel. The adventures you went on and the laughter you shared. Whether or not you lived your truth and pursued the things you were passionate about. If you were a good friend or parent or partner. If you left the world a slightly better place than how you found it. And none of those things have to do with the way you look.

I know there's so much pressure to be beautiful and live in a perfect body. And I know it can feel impossible to believe anything else when living in a culture that attached our lovability and worth and morality to how we look. But the truth is that it's not your job to be thin or attractive or visually appealing to anyone ever. You aren't here to sit around and look pretty or fuckable. You're here to get shit done. To make a difference and make a life. To experience what it means to be alive and enjoy the short time you have on this planet.

You have infinitely more to offer the world than the way you look. You have a story no one else can share and a perspective only you can give. You have a unique combination of strengths and talents and insights. Things that you, and only you, can share. You have your love and your laughter and your thoughts and the way you make people feel. That's what people remember. That's what matters. And that's who you are. You're radiant and resilient and kind. You're smart and hardworking and strong in ways people shouldn't have to be. You're a light, and no matter what you look like or how your appearance compares to anyone else's, you are enough.

Today is a new day. Whatever happened yesterday is over. Whatever happened, it's okay to forgive yourself. You can't go back in time and undo the mistakes you've made or change your behavior, but you can decide what you do today. So instead of beating yourself up, figure out what you can do now to get closer to where you want and need to be. Ask yourself, "What worked yesterday? This week? This month? And what didn't work? Which things and people made me smile and feel hopeful? Which people helped me feel connected and seen and heard? And how can I recreate those moments and maintain those relationships? Which things hurt and made me feel small? Which people and spaces made me question my worth? And how do I remove or limit my exposure to them? What's stopping me from taking the next step? What's the underlying fear? And what's one thing, big or small, I can do to lessen that fear and get closer to where I want to be?"

Things are not hopeless or lost. You aren't a failure. You're human. Mistakes happen. Struggles are inevitable. And what happened yesterday doesn't have to dictate what you do today. You get to choose again. You get to walk down a different path.

So much of what keeps us stuck in our fear is the "What if?"
What if I fail? What if things go wrong? What if I get hurt?
What if I get rejected?
What if it's difficult and uncomfortable?
What if I'm not strong enough to survive it?
What if my life is worse?

And those fears are valid.
They're real and debilitating, and the truth is that sometimes
what we're afraid of comes true.
Sometimes we fail and sometimes things fall apart.
But there's another side of the "What if?"
that we often forget about.
What if things go well?
What if your life gets better?
What if your life gets bigger and fuller?
What if you feel free?
What if you realize that all the things
you were afraid of weren't really so scary after all?
What if you thrive beyond
anything you ever imagined possible?
It's easy to get caught up in the worst-case scenario,
but sometimes we have to remind ourselves of the good
that can come. Because that's just as real and powerful.

—

DANIELL KOEPKE is a writer, clinical psychology doctoral student, and therapist in training. She is also the founder of a space called the Internal Acceptance Movement (I. A.M.), which seeks to promote mental health and foster self-acceptance. Her writing is guided by the concept of unapologetic vulnerability—giving people permission to honor their feelings as they come and to take up space in the world as their authentic selves. She is a firm believer in the idea that vulnerability can be a superpower that connects us, eradicates shame, and helps us heal. For more information about Daniell and weekly quotes, you can find her on social media.

instagram.com/daniellkoepke
www.facebook.com/Internal.Acceptance.Movement
internal-acceptance-movement.tumblr.com

THOUGHT CATALOG Books

Thought Catalog Books is a publishing imprint of Thought Catalog, a digital magazine for thoughtful storytelling. Thought Catalog is owned by The Thought & Expression Company, an independent media group based in Brooklyn, NY which also owns and operates Shop Catalog, a curated shopping experience featuring our best-selling books and one-of-a-kind products, and Collective World, a global creative community network. Founded in 2010, we are committed to helping people become better communicators and listeners to engender a more exciting, attentive, and imaginative world. As a publisher and media platform, we help creatives all over the world realize their artistic vision and share it in print and digital form with audiences across the globe.

ThoughtCatalog.com | Thoughtful Storytelling

ShopCatalog.com | Boutique Books + Curated Products

Collective.world | Creative Community Network

MORE POETRY FROM THOUGHT CATALOG BOOKS

Your Heart Is The Sea
—Nikita Gill

The Strength In Our Scars
—Bianca Sparacino

Salt Water
—Brianna Wiest

It'll Be Okay, And You Will Be Too.
—Jeremy Goldberg

THOUGHT CATALOG Books

THOUGHTCATALOG.COM
NEW YORK · LOS ANGELES